A LADYBIRD 'EASY-READING' BOOK

'People at Work'

THE POSTMAN
and the Postal Service

by
VERA SOUTHGATE, M.A., B.Com.

with illustrations by
JOHN BERRY

Publishers: Wills & Hepworth Ltd., Loughborough
First published 1965

THE POSTMAN

Five hundred years ago, not many people in this country could read or write. Very few people wrote letters. There were no posting-boxes for letters and no postmen to collect and deliver them.

The King's letters were carried by a special messenger. He was called the King's Messenger. He wore a bright, red uniform because red was the royal colour. His hat was trimmed with one or more feathers.

The King's letters were called the Royal Mail. The King's Messenger rode on horseback. He carried the Royal Mail in a leather pouch.

HOW TO ADDRESS AN ENVELOPE CORRECTLY

Mr. C. Smith,
   6, The High Street,
      BOLTON,
         Lancashire.

Correct addressing calls for:

1   The name of the person to whom the letter is addressed.

2   The number of the house or flat, and the name of the street or road.

3   In some cases the name of the village or district.

4   The name of the POST TOWN in block letters (the POST TOWN is the town that makes the deliveries to the address on the envelope.) In some cases the POST TOWN is followed by the district number or initials and number.

5   The name of the county in which the POST TOWN is situated (except for addresses in London and certain other large towns).

In this carefully planned reference book, interesting and accurate information is given about the Postal Service, its history and its development to meet present day needs.

Even children whose reading experience is limited will be encouraged by the superb, full-colour illustrations and relatively simple text to find out for themselves about this vital service, and at the same time gain extra reading practice.

LADYBIRD BOOKS

UK | USA | Canada | Ireland | Australia
India | New Zealand | South Africa

Ladybird Books is part of the Penguin Random House group of companies
whose addresses can be found at global.penguinrandomhouse.com.

ladybird.com

Penguin
Random House
UK

First published 1965. This facsimile edition published 2016.

001

Copyright © Ladybird Books Ltd, 1965

Ladybird and the Ladybird logo are registered trademarks owned by Ladybird Books Ltd

The moral right of the author and illustrator has been asserted

Printed in China

A CIP catalogue record for this book is available from the British Library

ISBN: 978-0-241-24950-5

www.greenpenguin.co.uk

Many years later the King's Messengers began to be called post-boys. They carried other people's letters as well as the King's letters. They were still supposed to look after the Royal Mail first, so they still wore red uniforms.

Some of the post-boys walked and some of them rode on horse-back. They only travelled along what were the main roads in those days.

Every post-boy on horseback carried a post-horn which he blew three times in every mile.

Along the main roads, there were inns where travellers could eat or sleep. The post-boys on horseback needed fresh horses every twenty miles. They used to stop at the inns, to eat and to change horses.

The inns where the post-boys stopped were called post-houses. They were about twenty miles apart. A post-horn over the door showed that an inn was a post-house.

The innkeepers of the post-houses became postmasters. The post-boys left some letters with the postmaster and collected other letters from him.

As time went on, more people gave letters to the post-boys. More roads became post roads and the post-boys' mail-bags became bigger and heavier. As their bags grew heavier, the post-boys became slower.

The highwaymen often waited to rob the post-boys. A highwayman usually wore a mask over his face and he rode a fast horse. He would snatch the mail-bag from the post-boy and ride quickly off with it. Later he would open the letters and steal any money that was inside them.

As more highwaymen robbed the mail, people became afraid to send their letters by post-boys.

Stage-coaches travelled along the same roads as the post-boys. They travelled much more quickly than the post-boys.

In 1784 some bags of mail were put on a stage-coach travelling from London to Bristol. It did the journey of one-hundred and twenty miles in seventeen hours. This was very fast travelling in those days.

Soon nearly all the mail was being sent by mail-coaches, instead of by post-boys.

The mail-coaches were beautifully painted and polished. Each coach was pulled by four very fine horses.

A guard sat at the back of every mail-coach. He wore a royal uniform of red and gold and a tall hat. He carried a large, brass post-horn which he often blew. The guard also had a gun and two pistols, to guard the Royal Mail against highwaymen.

One of the fastest of the mail-coaches was 'The Bristol Flyer'. By 1816, it could travel from London to Bristol in less than twelve hours.

It was very exciting when a mail-coach arrived at a post-inn. Grooms ran to the stables to bring out fresh horses. Servants rushed about with food and drinks for the passengers.

The guard handed over a bag of letters to the landlord and collected another bag from him.

Then on went the mail-coach, often driving during the night. At each post-house on the road, the guard delivered bags of mail and collected others. Sometimes this was done from an upstairs window, without the guard getting down from the coach.

At this time, letters were not put in envelopes. They were just folded over and sealed with hot wax. The letters did not have stamps on them.

There were no posting-boxes in which to post letters. People had to take their letters to posting-houses, to be collected. In big towns, letters could be given to a man called a letter carrier. He went through the streets ringing a bell.

Letters were not delivered to people's houses as they are now. They were left at the posting-houses for people to collect.

For many years the Royal Mail travelled by the fast mail-coaches. Then steam engines and railway trains were invented. The trains travelled much faster than coaches.

In 1830 a mail-bag was first carried on a train from Liverpool to Manchester. It travelled much more quickly than if it had gone by mail-coach.

Soon more railways were built in this country. Then more and more mail was sent by rail instead of by mail-coaches.

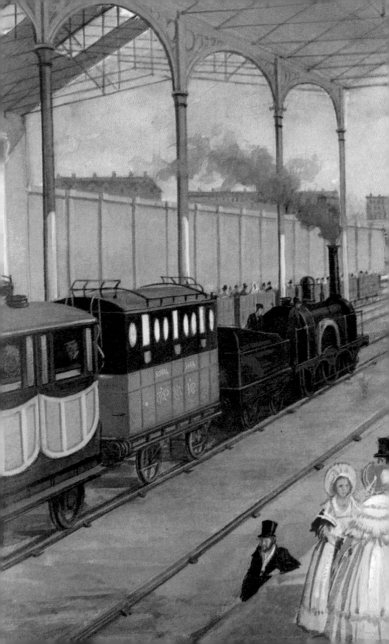

During the next hundred years many more letters were written. Collecting and delivering the mail were made easier.

Posting-boxes were set up in all the towns and villages. (The picture shows the first posting-box which was set up in a street in 1855.) Now no one need walk very far to post a letter.

To-day letters are delivered to everyone's house by postmen. The postmen wear navy blue uniforms with red pipings. These narrow red lines remind us that postmen still carry the Royal Mail.

LETTERS
LETTER BOX
POST OFFICE
LETTER BOX
N°2
0 · 7 178
FROM CENTRAL POST OFFICE

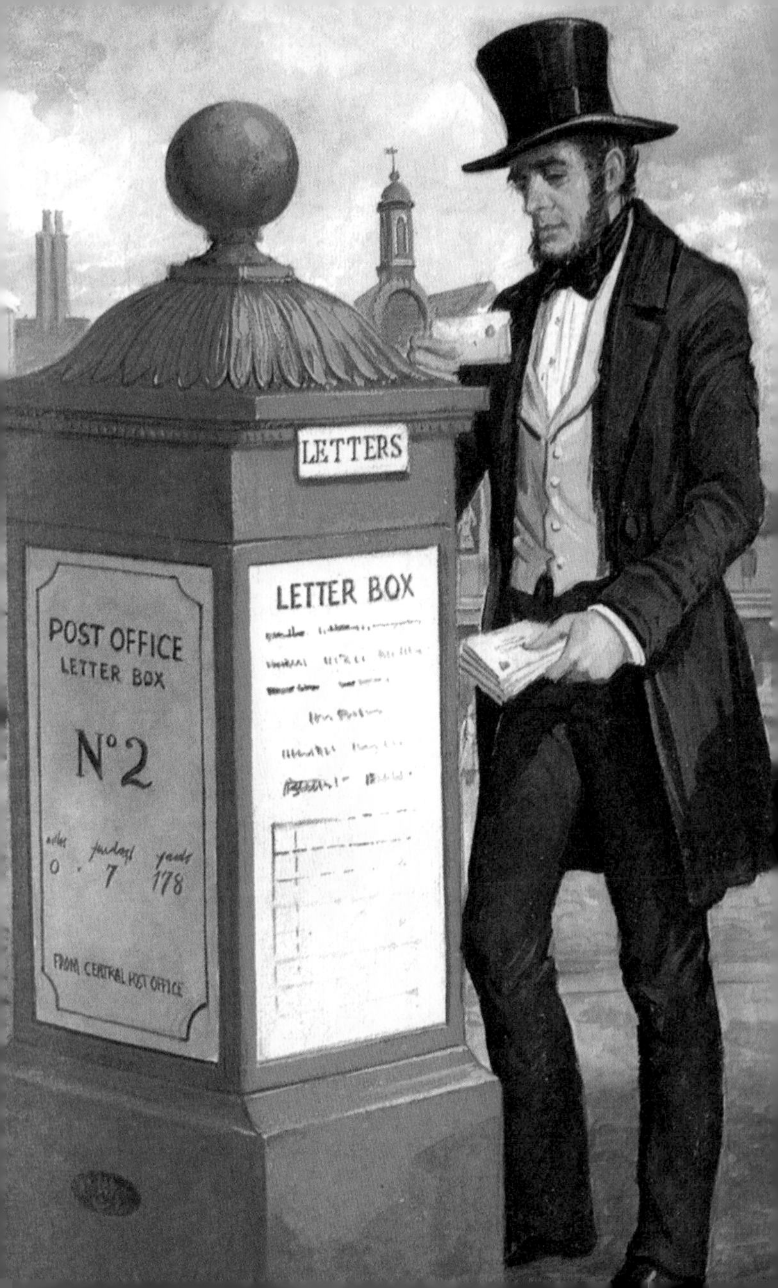

Every day, about eight-hundred thousand parcels and twenty-six million letters are posted in this country. Let us see how the mail reaches the people to whom it is sent.

First of all we buy stamps, for our letters and parcels, at post offices or from stamp machines. Then we post the letters in posting-boxes. There are about one-hundred thousand posting-boxes, spread all over the country.

Small parcels can also be posted in posting-boxes. The General Post Office (G.P.O.) call these small parcels, 'packets'. Large parcels must be taken to post offices to be posted.

The letters and packets are collected from the posting-boxes by postmen. This work is called 'clearing' the boxes. It is often done by postmen who drive small red G.P.O. vans.

The postman carries a key to open the door in the side of the posting-box. He puts all the letters and packets from the box into his bag. Then he changes the time on the little label, to show people when the box will next be cleared.

In busy towns the posting-boxes are cleared many times every day. In more lonely places, the boxes are cleared only once a day.

The mail collected from the boxes is taken to a large post office to be sorted. The mail-bags are emptied on to a big table. The letters, postcards and packets are all mixed up in a big pile.

First the letters have to be separated from the packets. This job is called 'segregating' the mail. A man called a sorter stands at the table and segregates the letters and packets. This must be done first because the packets cannot go through a stamp-cancelling machine.

Next the small letters are separated from the large letters. Then the letters are 'faced'. This means that all the letters are turned the same way. The addresses must be on top, and the stamps in the top right-hand corner.

When the letters have been segregated and faced they go through a stamp-cancelling machine. The machine cancels the stamps by putting a postmark on them. This is done to stop people using the stamps again.

The postmark shows the date, the time and the town in which the letter was posted.

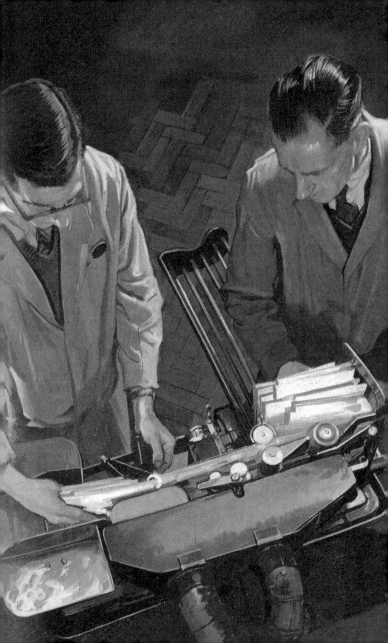

Next the letters are sorted on a sorting frame. It looks like rows of shelves, divided into open boxes. There are forty-eight boxes and they are called pigeon-holes. Each one has a label showing the name of a big town or a large district.

The sorter works in front of the sorting frame, so that he can reach all the pigeon-holes without moving. He looks at the name of the town in the address on each letter. Then he sorts the letters by putting each one into the correct pigeon-hole.

It is very important that letters should be addressed clearly so that the sorter can sort them quickly.

After the first sorting, the letters in each pigeon-hole are sorted again, on other sorting frames. The labels on these pigeon-holes are for much smaller towns and districts.

In some of the bigger sorting offices, the sorting of letters can be done by machines. One man working a machine can sort many more letters in the same time.

The letters are now ready to begin their journeys. The place to which a letter is going is called its destination. Letters for the same destination are tied into a bundle, and all bundles to that destination put into mail-bags. The bags for different destinations are tied up and sealed.

Most of the mail-bags are loaded into vans and driven to the station. There the mail-bags are put on to different trains for their destinations.

Mail-bags for nearby post offices are taken there in mail-vans.

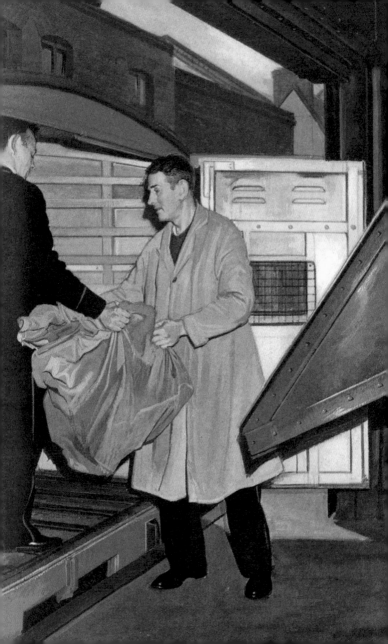

Some of the mail travels on ordinary trains. But a lot of the mail travels on special mail-trains. The mail-trains are fitted out as Travelling Post Offices. They have large sorting offices, fitted with proper sorting frames. G.P.O. men work at sorting the mail while the train is travelling.

During the night the mail-trains travel at high speeds. Then mail, from one end of the country, can be delivered at the other end of the country on the following day.

Mail-trains can collect and deliver bags of mail without stopping. Special metal arms stick out from the sides of the mail-coaches. Leather pouches of letters are hung on the metal arms.

At the side of the railway track, there is a special net. As the train passes, the net snatches the pouch of letters from the side of the train.

Further along the track, other pouches of letters hang on metal arms. These are letters for the train to collect. As the train passes, these pouches are scooped into nets on the side of the train.

In London there is a special Post Office Underground Railway. It runs seventy feet below the streets of London. Mail-bags travel on this railway from the sorting offices to the big stations. Small electric trains are used to carry the mail-bags.

This underground railway works very like a toy electric railway. The trains stop at stations but there are no drivers or guards. The trains are controlled electrically by a man who moves switches to make the trains stop and start.

In places, the tunnels are only eight feet wide.

Many of the letters, which are written in this country, have to be sent to destinations in other countries. The mail-bags for abroad are taken to airports or to seaports.

At the airports, the air-mail letters are put on to aeroplanes which fly all over the world. Nowadays, an air-mail letter can reach almost any place in the world in a few days. Some mail is also sent by helicopters.

The heavier mail for abroad goes by ship. Huge bags of mail are put into strong nets and swung on board the ships.

When the mail-bags arrive at sorting offices near their destinations, they are sorted twice on big sorting frames.

The postmen come to the sorting offices very early in the morning. They sort their letters ready for delivery. This sorting is called 'setting in'. Each postman puts the letters for his own delivery round into the order in which he will deliver them. It helps him to do this if the numbers of the houses are on all the letters.

As the postman does his setting-in he ties the letters into bundles and puts the bundles into his bag.

The letters are now ready to be delivered to their destinations.

The postmen set off. Some of them walk on their rounds, and some use bicycles. In country districts many of the postmen go out in mail-vans to deliver letters. On Dartmoor the postman rides on a pony to deliver his letters.

Letters to people in lighthouses, or people who live on small islands, are delivered by boat. Letters to people on ships, in the rivers or harbours, are also delivered by boat.

The busiest time of the year for the postman and G.P.O. workers is the few weeks before Christmas. During these few weeks millions of letters, Christmas cards, packets and parcels are posted.

They all have to be sorted and delivered to our homes before Christmas Day. The staff of the Post Office work very hard at this time of the year.

We all love to see the postman delivering Christmas mail to our houses. We wish him a "Happy Christmas" and thank him for delivering our mail safely during the year.

mail-van

sorter

mail-train pouches

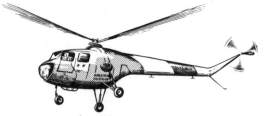

helicopter